NUMEROTARINA

THE NUMBER STORY

SMALL BOOK ONE

ENGLISH - FINNISH

*Numbers Teach Children
Their Number Names*

written and illustrated by

MISS ANNA

Early Reader Edition of *The Number Story 1*
Bronze Medal Winner, 2016 Wishing Shelf Book Award

Library of Congress Control Number: 2018902040

Names: Miss Anna, author.
Title: Number story : numbers teach children their number names / Miss Anna.
Description: Portland, OR: Lumpy Publishing, 2018.
Identifiers: ISBN 978-1-945977-39-8| LCCN 2018902040
Summary: The pictures and rhymes present stories which introduce numbers 0-10.
Subjects: LCSH Numeration—English--Finnish--Pictorial works--Juvenile literature. | BISAC JUVENILE NONFICTION /
Languages: English--Finnish
Classification: LCC QA141.3 .M57 2018 | DDC 513—dc23

Publisher: Lumpy Publishing
Website: www.missannabooks.com
Email: missanna@missannabooks.com

Paperback: ISBN 978-1-945977-39-8
Printed in the U.S.A.   1 3 5 7 9 10 8 6 4 2

Tahdotko oppia
numeroiden nimet?

It is very easy and a lot of fun!

Se helppoa on ja hauskaakin!

Say-along our little jingle

Laula kanssani loru tää.

starting from Number One!

Numero yhdestä lähdetään!

1
ONE looks like my one finger.

YKSI

on kuin yksi sormi.

1
ONE!
YKSI!

2

TWO trails a tail.

KAKSI

häntänä heiluu.

A TAIL! HÄNTÄ

3

THREE has bumps.

KOLME

on kuin kukkulalla.

BUMPY! KUKKULAT!

4

FOUR carries a sail.

NELJÄ

on kuin purje.

4
A SAIL!
PURJE!

5

FIVE   is a racing track.

VIISI

on kilpa-radan.

VROOM
VRUMM!
1

SIX   curves like a snail.

KUUSI

on kuin kiemura etana.

A SNAIL! ETANA!

7

SEVEN   has a sharp angle.

SEITSEMÄN

on erittäin terävä kulma.

OUCH!
AUTS!

8

EIGHT   is rollercoaster rails.

KAHDEKSAN

on vuoristorata.

JIPPII!
YIPPEE!

NINE is a bubble on a stick.

YHDEKSÄN

on tikussa kupla.

A BUBBLE! KUPLIA!

TEN   is an eye of a whale.

KYMMENEN

on valaan yksi silmä.

WINK!
VINK!
HELLO! HEI!

And
Ja
0
ZERO   is an empty pail.
NOLLA
on tyhjä saavi.

IT'S EMPTY!
AIVAN TYHJÄ!

Thank you for playing with us today.

We had a lot of fun too!

Kiitos kun leikit kanssamme tänään.

Meilläkin hauskaa oli!

We are your Number friends,
Zero to Ten,
Who will be here for you~

Nollasta kymmeneen ystäviä kaikki,
valmiina leikkimään~

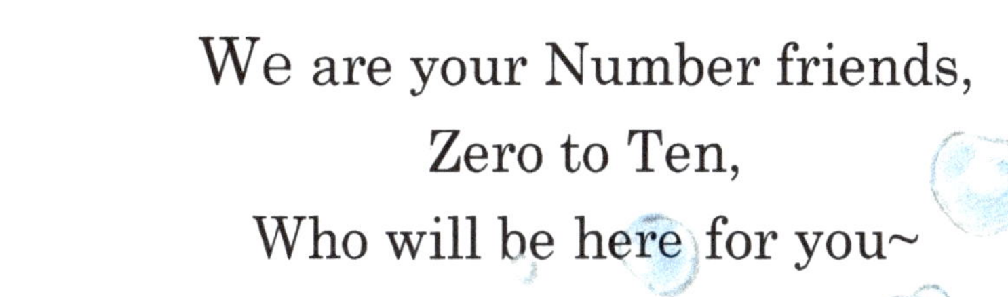

Bye-bye now!
See you again soon!

Hei hei nyt!
Tulethan uudestaan!